KEEPING IT REAL

A Six-Principle Approach to Something Different

Change • Reentry • Success

I0081206

EDWARD BALL

This is a Ball Team Enterprise LLC Publication

BALLTEAM
Enterprise , LLC

ISBN: 978-0-9899864-5-8

Keeping it Real class summer 2016

Contents

Introduction

"Keep it real!" What does this term mean? What does being and keeping it real mean? Unfortunately, the definition of *real* varies from person to person and region to region. In fact, according to some groups, there's just a small segment of people who can be considered real or eligible to keep it real. For example, people in 'hoods across America use this term to describe someone in the streets whose livelihood is crime. A criminal is *real*, but a hard-working law abider isn't even considered real. They are viewed as lame or square.

I have no idea what criteria the 'hood is using to determine an individual's realness; however, at one point I was considered real. I sold crack, smoked weed, didn't want to keep a job, carried pistols, shot people, committed robberies and home invasions, and partook in all sorts of unspeakable things, but I was so-called real. I even put crack in the hands of kids who were ultimately sent to prison, but I was real. I don't understand how I was real.

I prefer to use more inclusive criteria—one where everyone has the opportunity to be real. Your grandma, the mail man, the guy working the McDonald's drive-thru, and even a brotha in the hood. Adhering to the criteria found in this book is what I call 'keeping it real.' On the other hand, an unwillingness to adhere to these principles—like many criminals—makes you the opposite of real.

There are six basic criteria outlined in this book which must be applied before a person can be real and ultimately keep it real. Personifying these principles will lead to success in all walks of life. For those who are making transitions in life—like going from high school to preparing for college, people transitioning from thug to gentleman, or someone transitioning from a prisoner to citizen—recognizing and adhering to these principles is crucial to making a successful conversion.

Each of the six criteria are tied to six traits that were identified as keys to success by Stanford MBA Professor Jeffrey Pfeffer. This book points out how my keeping-it-real principles work with Professor Pfeffer's keys to success and can lead to successful transitions.

The criteria, which make up what I call the Real Matrix, consists of the following:

1. Accountability

2. Responsibility

3. Prioritizing

4. Self-advocacy

5. Respect

6. Self-efficacy

The keys to success related to the criteria in our *Real Matrix* include:

- Stamina

- Focus

- Sensitivity to others

- Flexibility

- Ability to tolerate conflict

- Submerging the ego

Fortunately, for anyone looking to make a successful transition, keeping it real is actually quite simple. Our parents have taught us everything found within this Real Matrix. By teaching us about respect, accountability, responsibility, and the other principles within my matrix, parents were not only teaching us how to keep it real, but they were also teaching us the keys to success.

This may seem strange, but those involved in crime and the street life—at least in theory—value many of the principles found within our matrix. Remember the No Snitching campaign? That campaign was about accountability. In summary, the campaign was telling people to be accountable for their own actions as opposed to telling on someone to limit or negate the consequences of those actions. Familiarity should make it easy for people to relate to the criteria in our matrix. One of the objectives of this book is to help those in a state of transition to clearly see a couple of things. First, they need to realize they've already been using these criteria and keys to success in their daily lives. Secondly, they need to know utilizing these principles can and will lead to a successful transition.

After reading this book, you will be able to:

- See the importance of the six principles as they relate to making a transition.

- Learn how these principles relate to the six keys of success.

- Better understand how to utilize these principles, increasing the likelihood of making a successful transition.

This book will also challenge your thought process. It's designed to change the way you see things and give you a new perspective of the principles outlined in this book. I have also included some real-life stories to help make the subject matter more understandable.

Things To Do Before You Read

Answer the following questions:

1. Where do you see yourself in the future?

2. What competencies do you lack that are keeping you from realizing that future?

3. What can and what will you do to acquire the necessary competencies to realize the future you see for yourself?

Chapter 1
Self-efficacy

Prior to going to prison, I didn't know how to do anything. I really never had a job, I hadn't taken up any trades, nor was I ever involved in any internship programs. All I wanted to do was ride, smoke weed, and sell drugs. My world was limited to a few city blocks.

After changing my perspective, I began to develop ideas about what I wanted to do and what I wanted to be once released from prison. Somewhere along the way, I was inspired by Robert Kiyosaki to become an author. I was reluctant to share my dream, because prison is like the army; you can be all you can be. Everybody in prison is a baller, pimp, and a killer. Once they get out, they are going to ball even harder, pimp even stronger, and kill any sign of an opponent. Telling people I was going to write a book was no different than a convict telling some woman on the phone he's going to get out and marry her.

I remember telling a friend of mine I was going to write a book. He laughed and asked was I going to write a 'hood novel. I laughed and told him I was going to write a self-help book. I maintained my goal despite the fact I didn't know the first thing about writing a book. But, at one time I didn't know how to do anything but sale dope. I wasn't too good at that; however, I believed in my ability to learn and accomplish new things.

I watched hours of YouTube, read a few books, and figured out how to publish my books. They are now available in eBook and paperback formats at various stores, Amazon, Barnes & Noble, and iTunes to name a few places.

What is Self-efficacy?

Self-efficacy is belief in your ability to reach your goals. When I use the term self-efficacy, I'm referring to high levels of self-efficacy, levels so high that you don't allow your current competencies or your history to limit you or determine your future. Instead, you believe in your ability to learn and get things done. Furthermore, you're willing to take on challenges others won't attempt.

We all have the ability to learn and overcome. That ability allows us to create the future we desire for ourselves. You may see yourself as a pediatric doctor even though you're currently at the bottom of your high school class, from the worst neighborhood in your city, and don't have the slightest clue of what it takes to be a doctor.

Despite your background, you can still become a doctor and learn everything it takes to become a great one at that. You'll be in college for about eight years, so you better be prepared. Your past can't keep you from becoming that pediatric doctor unless you allow it. No patient will care two cents that you were at the bottom of your high school class or came from a housing project in a crime-infested neighborhood if you are a competent, educated, and a well-trained doctor. In fact, overcoming a tumultuous background makes you even better. Displaying high levels of self-efficacy entails going out and learning what you need to in order to be the version of yourself you visualized and utilizing your past to be the best version of self possible.

Don't rely on what you currently know. Don't use your past as an excuse. Don't be afraid to do something different. Finally, don't emulate the person with low self-efficacy levels who doesn't bother to set goals, settling for what they have always had: nothing but trouble.

Something to think about

Everyone has an imagination, some kind of goal, and something in their past that can be utilized for their own benefit. Additionally, everyone has learned something they felt they couldn't at some point and accomplished something seemingly impossible. As a result, everyone is capable of having a high level of self-efficacy.

You can roll through any 'hood and find someone who has a vision to be a big-time drug dealer or an ultimate thug. They are actively taking steps to see that vision manifest, risking their lives and freedom. The ability to paint a picture of what they want to be and then go after it is a trait that can be utilized to produce a sustainable and healthy future.

Why Having High Levels of Self-efficacy is Important:

I've encountered dozens of guys who left prison after many years only to return to the exact place and activities that landed them in the joint. From speaking with some of them, I learned a few things:

<u>They were unwilling to learn</u>

They knew what they knew and relied on that static knowledge base. They refused to learn new things in part, because it was difficult and time consuming. They couldn't see the rewards of learning something new.

<u>They didn't have a vision</u>

First, they never had any strategic plan outside of returning to their past lifestyle. Second, they didn't take time to see all the options they had in the outside world. As mentioned above, they were also unable to see what new doors could open as a result from learning new skills

<u>They blamed their past on outside forces</u>

Some of the guys thought learning anything new would be a waste of time, because they wouldn't be given any opportunities once people looked into their backgrounds. They used their backgrounds as an excuse to not learn, not change, not grow, and not go after new opportunities. Instead, they chose on settling for what they already knew and where they'd already been.

The important benefits of having high levels of self-efficacy include:

- Keeps you from becoming unwilling to learn

- Helps you create a vision

- Forces you to utilize your past as opposed to blaming it on someone or something else

Self-efficacy won't allow you to return to who you once were, but rather, it allows you to use who you used to be to make a successful transition into a bright future. I can't see myself running around the hood slanging dope, hanging with a bunch of dudes, smelling like weed, and wearing baggy clothes with bright letters across my chest and butt. Nevertheless, I will use what I've learned from my past to relate to those who are currently where I was. I believe it will help them to make their desired transitions.

Keys to Success: Energy and Physical Stamina

Learning new things, formulating a vision, utilizing your past, and attempting to change your life requires energy and stamina, both physical and emotional. People often give up too soon when they run into hard times, obstacles, and opposition. That's when you must become energized and keep pushing until you succeed. Countless people give up when a couple of doors shut in their faces and their friends are chastising them for not adhering to what and who they used to be.

I spent many hours learning how to use the various components necessary to make my vision of being a published author a reality. Then, I spent many more hours enduring trials and mistakes trying to actually use those components. Some of the mistakes during this process zapped my emotional and physical energy, and I had to find the vigor and stamina to keep going.

Whatever your goal is in regards to your personal transition, it's going to require drive and perseverance. If you want that particular job, you are going to have to get up, go out, make calls and visits, build connections, talk to people, knock on doors, write resumes, write cover letters, deal with rejection, bounce back stronger, and all of these things are going to take a physical and emotional toll on you. However, you'll have to find the power to keep pushing to attain success. Those who have the energy and stamina to keep it pushing will be the victors; those without it will be the ones right back at square one.

Conclusion

Some key points to take away include:

- Displaying self-efficacy is going out and learning what must be done in order to become the best version of you. Utilizing your past can help you to become the greatness you've visualized.

- Overcoming a tumultuous background makes you even better.

- Self-efficacy doesn't allow you to return to who you were, but it allows you to use who you used to be to make a successful transition into a brighter future.

- Attempting to hide your past or devaluing your experiences is a mistake.

- Learning new things, formulating a vision, utilizing your past, and attempting to change your life requires energy and stamina.

Follow-Up

1. Where do you see yourself in the future?

2. What competencies do you lack that are keeping you from actualizing your best future?

3. What can and what will you do to acquire the necessary competencies to attain the future you see for yourself?

4. Outline a list of things you need to learn in order to make your transition successful.

5. Do you think you have the success trait associated with this principle?

6. If so, how do you plan on utilizing that trait to make your transition successful? If not, how can you compensate for that shortcoming in order to make your transition a success?

Things To Do Before You Read

- What does prioritizing mean to you?

- Determine what your priorities are in making successful transitions, and write them down.

- Begin thinking about how properly prioritizing can help you move forward.

Chapter 2
The Ability to Prioritize

I hadn't seen my running buddy, Black, in nearly sixteen years. I was in maximum security prisons and he was in and out of lower-level facilities. By the time I came home, he was doing another prison sentence. Almost two years after my release, Black got out of prison on a summer Monday morning. He was back slanging dope by Wednesday.

I ran into him on a Friday. His attire caught my eye. Just from listening to him, I began to understand his situation. He had on a $200 pair of grey, blue, and florescent-green Nikes, an $80 pair of gray, crispy new Levis that he sagged like a youngster, a hundred-dollar ball cap to match his outfit, and a pocket full of dope money.

From my point of view, Black's situation was dire. He had no job and wasn't looking for one. He had no place of his own to live, no car, and had multiple children to take care of. He was staying with some hoodrat in a criminalized, doomed neighborhood, borrowing her car, and slanging dope in the same place that had landed him in prison.

In my opinion, Black was the personification of the inability to prioritize. Let's not even talk about the drug dealing in a criminalized hood where he was the usual suspect. Let's stick with the message conveyed by his outfit. Why would you spend more than $300 on an outfit when you are essentially homeless, have no way to get around, unemployed, and you're on parole? A person with a basic understanding of prioritizing would've used that money to find a job, a place of their own, and a car to get back and forth to work and satisfied the demands of parole.

What is the Ability to Prioritize?

Having the ability to prioritize means you can effectively determine the order of dealing with *things to do*, according to their importance.

Black, like many of us, had an inability to effectively prioritize on a consistent basis. We might get it right sometimes—hopefully when it counts—but we'll get it wrong sometimes.

Black, however, seemed to have it wrong on a fundamental level. Looking at Maslow's hierarchy of needs, Black put his most basic needs in someone else's hands, particularly the needs associated with safety—security of body, employment, health, morality, family, and property. By getting involved with drugs, hanging in a criminalized neighborhood, living with a hoodrat, and refusing to look for sustainable employment, Black put his esteem before his safety needs. To Black, feeling good, looking good, and having the respect of the 'hood was more important than his freedom, health, and providing for his family.

On a basic level, those with just an inkling of the ability to prioritize will make sure their basic needs are met. A sustainable source of income is vital, because it allows you to pay for the other basics like food, shelter, and clothing. A problem exists when rent money is spent on Nikes and the unemployed buy expensive clothes that are unsuitable for a job interview.

I was released from prison to a work release center after more than a decade in prison. I didn't have much. My number one goal was to get a job. My basic needs were met in part. I had a place to sleep, about six pairs of clothes I could wear, and at least three sack lunches a day. Once I secured a job, I used some money I'd saved and borrowed to purchase a car, so I could get back and forth to work to keep my job. After that, I began working on my credit, realizing that a good credit score is vital to access other resources like housing. At no point did I go hang in a den of crime, buy Air Jordan's, or purchase drugs. I prioritized somewhat effectively, though at times, I did spend money on fast food and hung out with friends as opposed to saving that money for something relative to my career or life progress. Nevertheless, I effectively determined the order of dealing with things I had to do according to their order of importance, and that's what prioritizing is about.

Something to think about

I met a guy in the joint named Money. He was doing a sentence for dealing drugs—weed specifically. A year after we met, he was up for release. His plan was to reconnect to his old life and start up his drug business again. Money had a sense of what his priorities were. He understood that he needed some sort of income in order to eat, have a place to sleep, clothes to wear, and pay fees related to his parole. Most people understand prioritizing, like Money and Black; however, everyone isn't able to prioritize effectively and consistently. This is due, in part, to their self-efficacy levels and their ideals regarding their current competencies. In other words, all they knew was drugs and crime. They didn't believe in their ability to learn new things and to be successful at what they learned.

Why Having the Ability to Prioritize is Important:

Prioritizing is important because:

- It's a marketable skill

- It saves time

- It's vital to goal realization

Marketable skill:

The organization I currently work for uses standard questions during the interview process to determine a candidate's ability to prioritize. Some organizations do a credit check on applicants. From that check, they can determine a few things I've talked about in this book. They can get an idea of the applicant's level of accountability, how responsible they are, how they choose to allocate their scarce resources to meet their wants and needs, and how they prioritize.

Individuals who can demonstrate a pattern consistent with having their priorities in order are more likely to get a job or the contract over someone who can't demonstrate the same.

Saves Time:

On the surface, crime and chicanery look like shortcuts to the finer things many desire in this life; however, when all is said and done, that shortcut actually turns into a longer road. Furthermore, that road will be filled with barriers.

Back in the day, Dre was the man in the hood. He was holding the drugs, T's, and Blues. He had the women, a nice car with hydraulics—almost unheard of at that time—and the fresh clothes. The lifestyle he chose took him down a long road filled with prison terms, drug use, dysfunctional relationships, poverty, and plain ole bad times. After more than thirty years, Dre has finally found something that resembles a normal life.

Keisha, on the other hand, worked for minimum wage at various fast food restaurants while going to school. She would barely speak to any dude in the streets let alone allow one to enter her life. Keisha secured her normal life in ten years—a life where she owns a house, has good credit, a traditional family, and a successful career.

Dre's normal life meant working a job that kept his head just above water, owning a used car he worked on to keep running, and renting from a slum lord. He didn't have a savings account or a retirement account like Keisha, nor did he have a degree or a traditional family. Keisha prioritized properly and didn't waste decades of her life taking shortcuts. Your transition process can stall or go backwards if you fail to prioritize effectively.

Goal Realization

Keisha had a goal. The items that were prioritized played a role in helping her reach her goal. Dre, on the other hand, allowed many unimportant things to become a priority. I don't think he had a goal to begin with.

I wanted to write a book that would sell. I was working for eight bucks an hour, was broke, on parole, and had no idea what I was doing. I literally sat in the house all summer. I didn't hang out, go out, or shop. Everything I did was relative to helping me reach my goal of becoming a published author. Sure, I wanted to go enjoy my first summer as a free man. I wanted to go hang out in the sun. I wanted to go out and chase girls at the nightclub. However, none of that would've helped me reach my goal. In fact, it would've slowed me down or even derailed me from reaching my goal altogether.

GETTING YOUR PRIORITIES IN ORDER IS MANDATORY!

Key to Success: Focus

A very important success trait is focus. Jeffery Pfeffer describes focus as making decisions in the present that are in accord with your long-term goals.

Dre lacked focus. He lacked focus because he had no vision. How can you make decisions in line with your long-term goals if you have no real concrete, long-term goals?

Keisha was focused and had a vision. Every decision she made was centered on her goals of being educated, landing a career, and becoming financially stable.

If your goal is to transition from a high school student to a young adult in college, from the streets to the workplace, or from prison to society, the key is remaining focused. This means prioritizing activities that will help you make that transition successfully.

I decided very early during my prison sentence that I wanted to get out as soon as possible and with skills that would secure me a job or allow me to create a viable business. I focused hard. I went to college in prison for six years. I went to two vocational courses that took over three years. I took two, two-year courses via mail. I studied, read, wrote, and most importantly, I imagined my success, even while locked up.

I didn't involve myself in things that jeopardized my early release. I also stayed away from behaviors that would make me unemployable after my release. I didn't chase drugs, didn't run with a clique, didn't thump on my chest, and I didn't worry about the trifles that went on in prison. I realized those things wouldn't help me get out or find a job. Not one employer or business partner has ever asked me if I was the baddest convict in cell block four. However, they've asked me what I've done since my conviction. Luckily, I had the focus to prioritize my education over getting high to forget the fact I was sentenced to forty years in prison. If I can focus and prioritize in and out of prison, you should be able to as well.

Conclusion

Increasing your ability to prioritize requires:

Sacrifice:

Spending years in educational programs while my cohorts were having fun drinking, smoking, and making money drug trafficking was a sacrifice. Keisha had to sacrifice immediate gratification such as clubbing and shopping in order to reach her goal.

Focus:

Make decisions now that align with whatever your long-term goals are.

Put the things that are going to help you be successful first. If it doesn't contribute to helping you reach your goal, whether that goal is to make a seamless transition or become financially stable, put it at the bottom of your list or get rid of it altogether.

Follow-Up

1. What does prioritizing mean to you?

2. Determine what your priorities are using

something like Eisenhower's Urgent/Important Principle or our priority scale.

3. How can utilizing this principle help you attain a successful future?

4. Do you think you have the success trait associated with this principle? If yes, how do you plan on utilizing that trait to make your transition successful? If no, how can you compensate for that shortfall in order to make your transition a success?

Things To Do Before You Read

- What does being accountable mean to you?

- What do you think it would take to successfully implement accountability in your life?

- Begin thinking about how being accountable can help you move forward.

Chapter 3
Accountability

Back in the day, I had a dope fiend rental, which basically is a car rented in exchange for crack. It was a big red Suburban. I had picked up a chick from one of the surrounding neighborhoods, one of my running mates, and a guy we did drug deals with. We were driving through the neighborhood around the corner from our crack houses. The first time we came through the neighborhood on the way to this yellow row of houses where we sold crack, I noticed two guys from a rival neighborhood sitting in a black, late-80s-model, gas-guzzling car. After a brief stop at the crack house and some weed rolling and smoking, we piled into the Suburban, headed to the west side of town.

I had my mind made up to do a drive-by on these guys sitting in the gas guzzler; however, I didn't tell my passengers what was about to occur. We came around a bend in the road going east. The rivals sat in their car facing west. I pulled next to them, just one lane away. They didn't react, perhaps because they didn't realize who I was or what was about to happen. The Suburban came equipped with window tint worthy of escorting the president. At that point in my life, I was always armed with a pistol of some sort; that day, it was a black .40-caliber Glock. I rolled down the window, and they reacted by hopping out of the car. The driver was first. He was in a better position to recognize me. The passenger followed, reacting like a herd of buffalo to the movements of one skittish buffalo who thought he saw a lion. By the time I got my pistol up and pointed out of the window, they were a few yards from the car in an open field. The passenger trailed the nimble driver of the gas guzzler. I released three or four shots and sped away not knowing the outcome of my actions.

A few months later, I was sitting in the county jail going through the pre-trial motions for this shooting, where one person was shot in the butt. To my surprise, I had a co-defendant in the case involving this drive-by. Unfortunately, my co-defendant had nothing to do with the drive-by at all! While my other cohorts and I were rolling around in the dope-fiend rental, he stayed at the crack house making money. However, because we were associated with each other, our rivals assumed we were together when they were shot at.

The victims told the police that my co-defendant was sitting in the backseat and handed me the gun I used to shoot at them. At this point, he was guilty until proven innocent, and it was our word against theirs. What happened next was my most memorable moment of accountability.

I was put in a precarious position. I wanted to fight the case since there was no evidence; however, I couldn't let an innocent man risk going to prison for something he had no involvement in. I was willing to take account for my actions. As a result, I admitted my guilt and my role in the drive-by. I testified for my co-defendant, who won his trial. I went to prison with a five-year sentence that was tacked on to the end of a thirty-four-year sentence I received several months later.

What is Accountability?

The definition I prefer to use for accountability is simple: the willingness to account for one's actions.

Even though I was compelled to be accountable in the above story, I never blamed anyone or outlined anyone else's role in that shooting. I didn't blame anyone or anything in any of the cases I ultimately went to prison for. I was the one who had gotten caught and I couldn't account for the actions of anyone else. I carried the entire load.

Being accountable means being willing to stand up and take the blame and the praise for your actions or your role without point fingers. This is very important, because we will all find ourselves in situations where we have to stand up and accept responsibility. At that point, many people will begin to make excuses and point fingers.

For example, imagine a father gets a call from school saying their child was involved in some malfeasance. When the child comes home, the father is ready to dole out a whooping as punishment for the child's behavior. The child says, "WAIT! You never listen to my side of the story!"

With a look on his face that suggested his mind was already made up the father retorts, "Let's hear what you have to say." With that, the child begins to recount how he wasn't involved in anything that went on and about how he was just in the wrong place at the wrong time and guilty by association.

The father switches to his *it's time to learn a lesson* voice and says, "That's all fine and dandy. I believe you; however, we are dealing with an entirely different issue." The child looks puzzled like a puppy trying to understand what his master is talking about. The father goes on after shaking his head, realizing the child doesn't get it yet, "You are getting this whooping because you allowed yourself to be put in a situation where the school has to call me! How many times have I told you to watch who you hang with and think about the possible outcomes of whatever you are or aren't doing?"

The child may not have realized it, but he has received a lesson in accountability. Whether he was directly or indirectly involved in the malfeasance didn't matter. He still had to be accountable for his role, no matter how small or insignificant. So it is with the lives of adults—no excuses or finger pointing, as all we can do is stand and account for our roles.

Something to Think About

The connection a criminal element has to accountability is interesting. In theory, accountability is a prerequisite for involvement in crime. Crime cannot be successful if no one is willing to stand up and take blame for their actions. In other words, everyone ends up in prison if everyone snitches.

Notice I said *in theory*. I have met few people who actually adhere to the prerequisite accountability synonymous with crime. They value the no-snitching rule; however, being accountable plays second fiddle to perceived self-interest. When criminals get caught, they often tell everything while expecting no one to tell on them.

People making a transition from prison to society or from the block to the workplace understand the concept of accountability.

Why Accountability is Important:

Accountability is extremely important, especially when we are talking about making a transition because it does at least three things:

- Keeps you in check

- Builds credibility

- Propels you forward

In Check:

Through my experiences, I've come to learn that people with low levels of accountability prefer to do whatever they want and tend to disregard the possible consequences of their actions. This is evident in today's criminal justice system—criminals commit all sorts of crime knowing all they have to do is tell on someone and they will get off unscathed, with probation, or with significantly reduced sentences.

Mainstream society is no different. People do all sorts of things they have no business doing. Once caught, individuals with low accountability blame others for their mistakes, crimes, and violations. They are so far removed from accountability until they defer to blaming their parents for raising them with some emotional need being unfulfilled. As adults, they're compelled to commit crimes, assuming these violations will somehow make up for a void left by their ill-equipped parents.

These exit doors that allow individuals to escape responsibility have created a culture of snitches, finger pointers, blamers, and adults supposedly raised by parents who've failed at their jobs. These people are out of check. They risk continuing criminal behavior to do whatever they want, then snitch, blame others and point fingers, so they don't have to endure the consequences of their actions.

People with high levels of accountability endeavor to keep their actions in check, acknowledging that they may suffer the consequences of their actions in full. If the cost of their actions outweigh the benefits, these individuals will not deliberately engage in the action. Violations are limited, and in some cases, non-existent. If involved in a violation, these individuals will not reroute blame or whistle blow. Instead, they will account for their role, even if that role was playing the fool who didn't see what was going on. In short, the difference between someone with low levels of accountability and high levels are as follows:

Low Accountability Levels

Behaves recklessly

Doesn't understand proportion

Blames, points fingers, snitches

High Accountability Levels

Behaves with care and thought

Understands the action/consequence correlation

Understands and accepts their culpability

Actions and behaviors are kept in line when you have to suffer the consequences of those actions and behaviors. They get out of whack when you know there's someone to throw under the bus and suffer in your stead. These behaviors are evident when parents get bills in their children's names. They run bills up because they know they aren't going to be held accountable. When the bill is in your name, you will sit in the dark, wrapped in a blanket, just to keep those bills manageable.

Who are people going to want to have as part of their network—someone out of check or in check?

Builds Credibility:

When people recognize one is willing to stand up and give an account of his/her actions, the likelihood of that person doing the right thing is increased. They are then identified as being more reliable and trustworthy than someone who is a blamer. Credibility allows people to move forward—a vital part of any transition process.

My record includes about ten felonies including criminal confinement and battery. From an employer's point of view, that is ugly. As you might imagine, finding a job was difficult and upward mobility was almost out of the question.

I was fresh out of prison after nearly fourteen years and in a work release program. I was given an opportunity, because I made it a point not to blame anybody else for my going to prison. I never cried about it; instead, I highlighted how I had turned my hard time into an opportunity to become better and acquire skills that might add value to an organization. I got a job making $7.25 an hour, of which 65 percent was taken by the work release center. Even still, I worked like I was making $50,000 a year in order to build my credibility. I was punctual. If I made mistakes, I admitted them and tried to learn from them. And, I behaved as a person who understood the relationship between my actions and the consequences of those actions.

Eventually, I got a raise and was making $7.62 an hour; 65 percent still went to the work release center. A few months later, I got another raise and was making $8 an hour. By this time, community corrections was taking $400 a month out of that meager salary. On top of that, my coworkers who had just started were making just as much as me; however, I still worked like I was making $50,000 a year.

That credibility paid off, and I was promoted to a position where high levels of accountability were required.

Accountability was a vital part of my transition from prison to society and from $7 an hour to a salaried management position.

Propelling Forward

Pointing fingers and blaming stops forward motion, and we can't successfully transition without moving forward. Pointing fingers and blaming keeps us from focusing on the roles we played in the matter and taking corrective action where we have the authority to do so.

When I was convicted of all those felonies, there were people who alerted the police of my crimes, testified on the stand, and even made videos implicating me in their assault. Keep in mind these were grown men who understood and benefited from the unwritten no-snitching rule. I had a hard time seeing past the roles they played in me getting sent to prison. For years, I was unable to take an honest look at the role I played in my going to prison, because I was more worried about their roles.

The moment I got over what they did—because I couldn't control their beliefs and actions anyway—I began seeing all the mistakes I'd made. I began to understand that my belief system was warped and had led to my criminal behavior. That understanding allowed me to take corrective actions. The strange thing is, I've been so busy trying to get myself right until I don't have time to blame, point fingers, or change what I have no power to change.

Blaming keeps you at a standstill. Most likely, it will cause you to move backwards. In order to move forward, you have to look at what *you* did and what role *you* played in your current and past situations. At that point, you can move forward, taking corrective actions as you transition from what you were to what you want to be. That's the power of accountability.

Key to Success: Flexibility

To be successful in your transition process, you have to be flexible. In other words, you must be willing to change your position and make changes when things aren't working. To be flexible, a component of accountability has to be present. For example, changing position or making changes when things are failing requires you to admit a previous mistake and take ownership of it. Making a transition is usually the result of having to change course—admitting and owning your previous error.

If you are honest and look at things critically, realizing that you need to be flexible should be simple, but actually doing so is another monster. However, just realizing that you need to be flexible is a step in the right direction. If nothing else, identify areas in your life where flexibility could be valuable.

As I sat in prison, I examined the 'hood, the people in the 'hood, belief systems in the 'hood, the dope game vs. working, dress codes, relationships and many other things. As a result, I stay away from the 'hood, have limited contact with people in the 'hood, work every day, dress in clothes that actually fit, and know the difference between friends, family, relatives, and enemies.

These minor adjustments have had a positive impact on my transition process.

Conclusion

Some key points to take away include:

- Be willing to account for your actions.

- If possible, understand your role at all times, so you know what you are accountable for.

- Don't point fingers, blame or snitch; doing so doesn't help you move forward.

- Keep yourself in check.

- Accountability will pay off—if not immediately, then down the road.

Follow-Up

1. What does being accountable mean to you?

2. How can utilizing this principle help you have a successful future?

3. Do you think you have the success trait associated with this principle?

4. If so, how do you plan on utilizing that trait to make your transition successful?

5. If not, how can you compensate for that shortfall in order to make your transition a success?

Things To Do Before You Read

- What does being responsible mean to you?

- Determine what your responsibilities are in making a successful transition and write them down.

- Begin thinking about how being responsible can help you move forward.

Chapter 4
Responsibility

I had a buddy named Danny. We met in a maximum security prison. He was serving a six-to-eight-year sentence for drugs. He stood just over six feet tall, weighed nearly 300 pounds, had a low cut with waves, and had a well-manicured beard. He reminded me of a teddy bear. He had taken his Shahada—the Muslim profession of faith—while inside and had great character and a gentle heart.

The phones in the prison cell house were attached to the wall about four feet off the ground with a two-foot cord. It was just long enough for us to sit on the floor and talk on the phone or bend slightly to stand and talk. There weren't any chairs, so we had to sit on the floor or stand. One day, Danny was using the phone, sitting on the floor with his back rested against the wall. He had just gotten off the phone with the mother of his daughter. After hanging up, he remained seated in the same place he had occupied while on the phone. He wore a look of sadness that barely concealed his fury. At the time, Danny didn't look like a man you wanted to ask questions. Later that day after he calmed and had time to reflect, he told me about his conversation that had left him simultaneously expressing woe and anger.

He had found out that his eleven-year-old daughter had engaged in a sexual relationship with a boy slightly older than her. He told me how she was an honor roll student in gifted classes, how proud he was of her, and how he believed her future was bright. His heart seemed to break as he went on to tell me that the boy had told everyone about the encounter and how she was being teased and called a hoe at school. Danny—and unfortunately countless others—was unable to tend to his responsibilities, because he is sitting in prison over the choices made. Being a parent is the ultimate responsibility; you are in charge of an entire life. Your duty as a parent is so important and vital that it should come before any and everything.

Danny sat helpless, unable to prevent his daughter from being hurt and unable to mend her wounds. He could not tend to his responsibility of protecting his daughter.

What is Responsibility?

To put it simply, responsibility is taking care of your obligations.

When I was released from prison, I had to depend on other people to get around or catch the bus. I was a slave to others' schedules and subjected to their moods. This wasn't going to work for me, because I had a responsibility to be places at a certain time. Fortunately, I had saved some money and my mother helped me out with the difference. With her assistance, I purchased a 1995 Toyota Camry with 185,000 miles for $1,500.

Purchasing the car caused a problem. I had to purchase a license plate and insurance in order to drive legally. I had been out of the loop for over a decade: no license, no insurance, and no real credit history. No major insurance company would give me car insurance. One company told me to try an online insurance company like Geico or Progressive. I called Progressive and it was a success. They were willing to give me the insurance I needed. Then, I ran into another problem: I didn't have a credit card or a debit card to pay for the insurance.

At this point, I was so frustrated and upset I almost pulled a 'hood move: going to the license branch with a bogus insurance number, so I could get my plates. Fortunately, I had a friend who talked me out of that and allowed me to pay her in cash, and she completed the transaction for me over the phone.

As a person with an obligation to obey the law and do things the way they are supposed to be done, I didn't drive the car until I was 100 percent legit. I had to park my car in my brother's driveway and catch the bus until I got insurance. That's what responsibility is about—doing what you have to do in order to take care of your obligations.

Something to Think About

All walks of life are familiar with responsibility, even your neighborhood thug. A drug dealer will give a lower-level drug dealer pounds of dope on consignment. He is trusting this other criminal to be responsible enough to not get caught transporting or distributing the dope by the police or robbers. In addition, he is trusting his fellow drug dealer to bring back a designated amount of money.

This process is repeated day in and day out with unbelievable success, which is indicative of a high level of understanding in some sense, when it comes to the concept of responsibility.

Why Responsibility is Important:

Being responsible is vital to making a positive change for many reasons. A couple of those reasons are:

- It keeps you out of trouble

- It opens doors

Keeps you out of trouble

Reflect back to my journey to acquire car insurance. If I hadn't jumped through all of the hoops to be a responsible driver, I would've opened myself up to all sorts of problems. I could've gotten in an accident, been pulled over, or been charged with falsifying documents. Then, I would've been jumping through different kinds of hoops: no car begging for a ride, no license begging for a ride, in debt begging for a dollar, or in jail begging for a visit.

I believe I've avoided trouble because I've done everything right and the way I was supposed to. The peace of mind knowing I was legit and had something in place to protect me from an accident kept me from needing to use that protection. People who are doing wrong often have to look over their shoulder. This makes them nervous and prone to making mistakes and causing accidents. With my license, I've gotten pulled over once or twice. Driving while suspended has gotten me pulled over and sent to jail three times as much.

No successful transition can be made if you are worried, doing the wrong things, and using your problem-solving skills to fight trouble instead of finding success.

Opens Doors

Coming home, I had nothing—no job, no real credit, no place to call home, no mode of transportation, no retirement, and no bank account. My girlfriend took me to her credit union and I opened a bank account for $10. One of my good friends helped me get a job. My family helped me get a car and a place to stay. They all knew I was a responsible person and would make the most out of their help. Being responsible opened doors to employment, transportation, and housing.

The people at the bank didn't know me from Adam. However, my check is deposited in their bank every two weeks for more than two years. I've gotten two credit builder loans and have consistently paid them on time. This pattern demonstrated to the bank that I am a responsible person. As a result, whenever I talk to the woman at the bank about money, she is in a hurry to give me much more than I asked for. Simply being responsible opened a door to money.

A door to upward mobility opened up at work because I was responsible. I came to work on time every day, did my job and then some, and I made decisions that reflected that I was a relatively responsible person.

You never know what may come as a result of being responsible.

Key to Success: Putting Ego to the Side

Ask any man in prison why he sold dope, robbed, or killed, and he just might say he did it for his children and/or family. Imagine that. This is the ego surfacing, and in some cases, it warps an individual's sense of responsibility. A responsible drug dealer guards and protects the dope and money while being an irresponsible parent by putting himself in a position to be removed from their child's life. How does a seemingly responsible drug dealer be irresponsible enough to be a drug dealer to begin with? Ego! People work hard every day to take care of their kids, so why do people slang dope to take care of their kids? Their egos prevent them from working at McDonalds or a warehouse, wearing Faded Glory (a Walmart brand of clothing), or driving a Corolla. They have to hang with the homies, wear Tru Religion, and drive that seven series on eights (a BMW with twenty-eight-inch rims).

To make a successful transition, the ego has to be locked away. It's the responsible thing to do. This is extremely true for those of us coming from a place when we had an abundance of disposable resources, to a place of uncertainty and scarcity. If you let it, the ego will whisper in your ear and you'll be back slanging dope and hitting licks to bring back the time when you were riding good, dressing good, and smoking good. When that happens, it's because one allowed the ego to take them backwards.

Prior to going to prison, I sold drugs. I never worried about how much something cost, never gave a thought about not having a hundred dollar pair of shoes, and I didn't worry about getting up every day and dragging myself to a job. In fact, doing those things was beneath me.

A part of my transition process meant practicing humility. I realized I couldn't go back to the drug money. I'd have to depend on a paycheck for a while. As a result, driving my Corolla, wearing a pair of four-dollar shoes, a Walmart shirt, and punching a clock every day is fine with me. Everything is still fine even after I see people who've been where I've been come home rolling brand new BMWs, wearing $200 pairs of shoes, and $300 jeans. My ego is in check and I remain responsible.

Don't allow ego to take you back to your pasts. Instead, be responsible and transition into what could be.

Conclusion

Some key points to take away include, but are not limited to:

- Take care of all the things you are responsible for.

- Responsible people acquire more opportunities than irresponsible people.

- Those who are responsible are more likely to stay out of trouble.

- Learn humility and control the ego.

Follow-Up

1. What does being responsible mean to you?

2. Write down what your responsibilities are in regard to making a successful transition.

3. How can utilizing this principle help you achieve a successful future?

4. Do you think you possess the success trait associated with this principle? If so, how do you plan on utilizing that trait to make your transition

successful? If no, how can you compensate for that shortfall in order to make your transition a success?

Things To Do Before You Read

- What does self-advocacy mean to you?

- Determine when self-advocacy may be necessary in making a successful transition and write them down.

- Begin thinking about how self-advocacy can help you move forward

Chapter 5
Self-Advocacy

A friend of mine called me one day and said a guy had approached her in an attempt to get in touch with me. She described who he was, and I realized it was a guy I will call O.G. I figured it was something important since he went through so much trouble to get my attention.

I tracked down his number and called him. He wouldn't say much over the phone. He insisted I come to his home and speak with him. I figured he might be interested in getting a job where I was currently employed. My next free day, I reluctantly went to his house. He lived in one of those criminalized, drug-infested neighborhoods I try to stay out of. We sat down in his dimly lit living room. Although I was anxious to find out what the heck he wanted, he seemed just fine with the small talk. After a few minutes, he finally told me why he called this clandestine meeting.

I was still in work release during that period of time, which made the contents of the conversation disrespectful, absurd, funny, and upsetting all at once. After nearly fourteen years in prison, O.G. had the nerve to tell me, "I have a million-dollar scheme!"

I had to hide my fury behind a look of stupidity. "Huh?" I responded. I leaned in closer to make sure I'd heard him correctly. I squinted to detect any sign of practical joking in his face.

He continued with a straight face, "My dude got a fool-proof hookup; I just need some real dudes!"

I continued to listen, anticipating him to bust out and say he was kidding. However, he didn't. Instead, he said, "We all goin' to eat when it comes through."

He never gave me too much information about what he thought he had a line on; however, I determined he was honest-to-God serious. I was so stunned all I could whisper was two words: "I'm cool." Then, I left in disbelief.

On our journey to improve, change, and transition to a new stage in our lives, we will encounter people from our past who need to be re-educated as to who we are today and how that person differs from the person we used to be.

What is Self-Advocacy?

Self-advocacy is speaking up and standing up for yourself in a manner that educates those you come in contact with on how to properly interact with you.

I was so upset and dumbfounded by my conversation with O.G. that I missed the opportunity to educate him on how to interact with the man who was sitting in front of him as opposed to the kid he used to know.

Education can come in multiple forms. I only know how to use two. First, you can flat out give someone a quick lesson. For example, not too long after I went to work release, I went to visit some people I knew. These were some stone cold alcoholics. It was mid-day, sunny, and it was hotter than an oven outside. Yet, these dudes were pissy drunk and still drinking. One guy had a clear cup of something that look liked kerosene. He had the audacity to offer me some by swirling the cup around near my face. At that point, I had to decline his offer with commentary. The commentary consisted of me informing him that I currently didn't drink, had no desire to drink, and would appreciate it not being put in my face.

The second way to educate people is by your actions—that is, living what you are preaching. One of my partners named Ball was recently released from prison and is in work release. We kick it and educate each other on who we are today compared to who we were back in the day. I was scrolling through my Facebook page, and I saw him in a picture with dudes who are involved in things opposite of the image Ball portrayed. I immediately began to think he was on his way back to the life he once lived simply because of that one photo. I may claim to have changed, but my claims will be unbelievable if you see me hanging in the 'hood with super thugs.

Education works best when you reinforce quick lessons with congruent actions. If you tell someone you are changing, if you tell them you don't do the things you used to, then your actions have to be in line with those claims.

Something to Think About

Today's popular counterculture is familiar with a form of self-advocacy. They call it *checking*. If someone disrespects you or makes an erroneous assumption about who you are, what you have done, or will do, custom dictates that you check that person or put them in their place. I liken it to the challenges issued in the 16th-19th century. If someone was dishonored, they sought satisfaction by throwing down the gauntlet and challenging the offender to a duel. Checking someone, putting them in their place, or getting on their top is more of a challenge than an exercise in education.

How to properly check someone needs to be taught and perhaps rebranded as self-advocacy. I still struggle with properly educating someone after they've made an erroneous assumption by suggesting I engage in activities that aren't in line with my transition. When O.G. came at me with his million-dollar scheme, I wanted to jump up and say, *Who the f*** do you think I am? You b*** a** motha*****?* Well, you get it... I felt so disrespected, because after all I've been through, after he closed the casket on me in lieu of my sentence, after he witnessed how I was working hard every day not to return to where I came from, he thought I was stupid enough to go into partnership with him on some nonsense.

I couldn't think of an intelligent way to check him without taking it to the 'hood—a place I want to avoid in actuality and behavior.

Why Self-Advocacy is Important:

Self-advocacy is very important for at least three reasons:

- It debunks assumptions.

Self-advocacy is important, because people don't always know you. That is, old friends will assume you are the same old person they used to hang with. New friends will make assumptions about who they think you are. Teaching these people who you really are is imperative.

- It stops your so-called friends from taking you back.

If you are truly attempting to make some sort of transition from what you were or what you did to something bigger, better, and, different, self-advocacy is key. Old friends will have you back selling dope, drinking Wild Irish Rose, popping pills, and packing pistols if you don't speak up and stand up. New friends will also have you doing crazy stuff you've never done before. If you don't speak up and educate them, you may find yourself tied up somewhere with a ball stuck in your mouth. Efforts to change and transition are derailed all the time by people you associate with that you haven't educated and stood up to.

- It keeps you from being tempted.

Although I missed the opportunity to educate O.G., I've managed to educate many of my old friends and the people I encounter day in and day out. Self-advocacy is important when it comes to nipping things in the bud. People I've educated don't even bother to test the waters to see if I will be interested in any nonsense like pill popping or armed robbery. That's vital: not to even be tempted to do things that aren't in line with your transition or life goals. We all know how temptation can knock you off track.

Key to Success: Ability to Tolerate Conflict

In this world, we will have to fight. In other words, we will have to stand up for something. We may have to stand up often enough until people realize that we are willing to fight for what we believe in.

If you're afraid to tell people no, inform them of your change, your transition goals, or stand up for yourself in any circumstance, you will definitely fail at reaching your goals.

Prison was similar to a jungle. The weak were preyed upon, and the strong were left alone. Lions and other predatory animals will chase down and kill a buffalo that turns and runs. However, they will think twice about fooling with a buffalo that stands its ground and puts up a fight. Similarly, in prison, if you are unwilling to exchange physical blows, you're susceptible to fall victim to those who were willing to fight. However, if you were known to be willing to fight whoever for whatever reason, people would think twice about messing with you.

Just like prison or the jungle, the same will be true when you're attempting to change or go against what is considered the norm. If you're unwilling to fight, your friends will continue to put those drinks in your face and present you with absurd, get-rich, quick, criminal schemes until you give in. On the other hand, if you're willing to fight, people won't be willing to pull you into a direction opposite than the one you're setting for yourself.

If you plan on having a successful transition, you have to be willing to fight for it.

Conclusion

If you didn't take anything away from this chapter, be sure to remember the following:

- People don't always understand when you're changing and are undergoing a paradigm shift. All they see is who you used to be or who they think you are. Your duty is to let them know what it is.

- Be willing to fight every fight related to your success.

- If you fight, your chances for having a successful transition are increased. When people see you are willing to fight, they will stop tempting you and avoid conflict.

Follow-Up

What does self-advocacy mean to you?

1. How can utilizing this principle help you have a successful future?

2. Do you think you have the success trait associated with this principle? If so, how do you plan on utilizing that trait to make your transition

successful? If no, how can you compensate for that shortfall in order to make your transition a success?

3. Make a list of people you need to educate.

Things To Do Before You Read

- What is respect to you?

- Determine what role respect can play in making a successful transition and write it down.

- Begin thinking about how properly utilizing respect can help you move forward.

Chapter 6
Respect

George's favorite line was "They can't whoop me!" George was the younger brother of Rob. They were both sent to prison with fifty years sentences each for murder, at a relatively young age.

Despite allegedly murdering someone, they were good dudes and a pleasure to be around. They were silly and had an innate ability to make everyone around them laugh. George, however, was an asshole and more hotheaded than his older brother. George had high levels of accountability, and his favorite line was his version of being accountable for his actions.

George would rob someone of their dope or borrow money (well, commissary) and not pay them back. He would admit to doing it followed by, "They can't whoop me!" He had that might-makes-right view. He believed he could do whatever he wanted, because his victims couldn't beat him up.

I mention all of this to point out that George was disrespectfully accountable.

What is Respect?

Respect is about showing regard and consideration. When we talk about using the criteria above to make a successful transition, respect is vital. Being accountable, responsible, speaking up for yourself, and properly prioritizing all don't mean much if they aren't done with respect.

In this book, respect occurs when you show regard and consideration for the actors and circumstances that relate to the adherence of the previously outlined five principles.

Something to Think About

Some segments of society seem to think respect is a one-way street—a street going only in their direction. I remember running the 'hood, smoking weed, shooting up the 'hood, playing loud music, slanging crack in front of people's homes, and doing Lord knows what else. If anyone had anything to say about me devaluing their property by selling dope in front of it, shooting up their neighborhood, or keeping them up at night playing loud vulgar music outside their window, I took it as disrespect. My entire clique felt like we were the only ones in the 'hood worthy of respect. In turn, we were to be given the utmost respect unconditionally. Respect can't be understood or appreciated if it isn't reciprocated.

To increase the odds of a successful transition, people need to understand that respect is a two-way street. Things usually don't work correctly without consideration and regard being given.

Why Respect is Important:

Respect is an important aspect of life. Each principle needs to be carried out with respect or they are rendered void.

Respect and Self-efficacy

You have to respect what you've been through, what you currently know, and what the future can offer, and not allow your current competencies or your history to limit you and determine your future.

Attempting to hide your past or devaluing your experiences is a mistake. Your past needs to be respected, analyzed, and utilized to help make your transition into the future a success.

Likewise, living in the past or being completely caught up in the present is disrespectful to the future. The future is inevitable, and you should be preparing for the future by learning from your past, learning where you currently are, and always working to create the future you want. Your past, present, and your future deserves that much respect, and so does your transition.

Respect and Your Ability to Prioritize

You show respect to your priorities and your ability by taking care of your business in proper order and manner. For example, you don't spend the rent money on Mike Epps tickets, a new outfit, and drinks. You prioritized incorrectly. Likewise, you don't engage in criminal activity as your primary income and forego legitimate sustainable employment. You prioritized in the incorrect manner. I realize you may need to have money coming in to pay the bills and survive; however, you have to do what is supposed to be done in its proper custom. The proper custom is finding a job or a legitimate hustle.

Doing what you are supposed to within the proper means and in proper sequence renders desired results. At the end of the day, desired results are what's important. Going about things in the wrong order will leave you homeless, and going about things in the wrong manner will land you in prison!

Respect and Accountability:

Imagine you made a mistake or some sort of error on the job. The boss comes to you to find out what happened. You'd have no problem standing up and admitting the error was all your fault. However, you decide to do it in a George-like manner and tell your boss, "Yeah I did it! Is there something you plan on doing about it?"

You completely disrespected your boss and blew your accountability. The fact that you are willing to take blame for your actions no longer matters, because you can't do so in a respectful manner. Realize that your boss will find an opportunity to get rid of you.

I had a little homie named Nelly who was in work release. I had met him in a maximum security prison. Nelly secured a job at a location where one of my friends was a supervisor. The supervisor's name was Mark. Mark was a good dude. I did some time in prison with him as well. Nelly was the younger of the two. One day while at work, Mark caught Nelly on a cell phone after he was explicitly told by Mark not to use his phone during work. Mark told Nelly he could expect a write-up. Nelly finished up his call and put his cell phone away. I guess Nelly couldn't be accountable in a respectful manner. He tracked Mark down in the warehouse and calmly told him, "You can write that little sh** up, I ain'ttrippin'!"

Nelly's comment suggested that he was willing to be accountable for his actions; however, he was unwilling to do so respectfully. If I'm not mistaken, Mark sent Nelly home indefinitely, and Nelly was ultimately sent back to prison for being unable to maintain employment.

When Nelly told me this story, I got the impression he was bent out of shape because he saw Mark on his cell phone immediately after he told his crew not to be using their phones on the job. Nelly had failed to respect accountability on a couple of levels. First, he approached Mark on some George-type stuff. Secondly, he was worrying about what someone else was doing. Respecting accountability includes being accountable for *your* actions despite what other people are doing, getting away with, or how hypocritical they may appear. When you are able to focus on your role, you won't be upset that others aren't being held accountable and respond by disrespecting your boss or the person you see getting away with using their cell phone.

Respect and Responsibility

Respecting your responsibilities is simple. If you have a responsibility, take care of it and do it with joy. When you get that energy bill in the mail, pay it with glee; don't frown and tuck the bill under a stack of paper and avoid it. I'm happy I'm able to sleep in a warm house with running, potable water. I enjoyed it all month without being hassled, so when I have the opportunity to pay my bill, I am happy and look forward to another month of warmth and water.

How disrespectful is the following scenario: A man is required to pay child support for his daughter in the amount of $700 a month. He is upset and feels that his daughter's mother isn't maximizing his $700 for his daughter's benefit. If he wasn't worried about the consequences of not paying, he wouldn't give her a dime. Since he had to pay, he decides to get 70,000 loose pennies from the bank and puts it in a wheel barrel and dumps it on his baby momma's porch.

Respecting your responsibilities is important for many reasons. First, if you respect them, you will be given more. I got a small credit builder loan from the bank that I pay on biweekly with no complaint or hassle. Now, when I go in the bank, the woman tries to make me take money. She asks if I need money to buy a car, house, or just a personal loan. If I paid my loan on time every time but did it with complaint, complexity, displeasure, hassle, and haggle, the bank would most likely be hesitant about giving me another loan.

Secondly, showing respect to your responsibilities builds positive relationships. I have a positive relationship with my light bill, phone bill, internet bill, and any other bills. I enjoy my services and they enjoy me paying for them.

I met a small business owner who quit her job to run her business full time. Business was slow for a while, and her bills became more difficult to pay. She still paid them on time with a smile. When she asked the car lot if she could miss a couple of payments and possibly have her payment plan restructured, they were more than happy to accommodate, allowing her to keep her vehicle. She respected her responsibility and pleasantly paid her bill on time every time. Do you think your baby momma is going to give you a pass on a child support payment after you've dumped a million pennies on her porch?

Having these positive relationships and the option to be given more responsibilities will help you during your transition process.

Respect and Self-Advocacy

In the process of educating old friends and new friends about how to interact with you in a proper manner, you have to do it respectfully. How I wanted to educate O.G. was by telling him about where I've been and where I plan to be in the future while I kicked his ass. However, violence begets violence and disrespect begets disrespect. Relationships built on disrespect or that have a disrespectful undercurrent have the potential to disrupt your efforts to make that change you've envisioned.

You don't want to burn any bridges. Some people just get it wrong and come at you sideways with no harmful intent. Nevertheless, some of those people may one day be in a position to help you make a successful transition. They may be resources as you may be a resource for them. Maintaining bridges is important and you don't want to destroy them.

Key to Success: Sensitivity to Others

Being sensitive to others, recognizing what they want, and knowing how to communicate and influence them is very important in all aspects of life. As it relates to making a transition, you'll encounter many people—some friends and some family—who will attempt to influence you to do things inconsistent with your journey. When you do run into these people, you should know what their intentions are, how to talk to them, and how to influence them to keep it moving and refrain from attempts to drag you away from your mission.

Having the ability to recognize what people want and how to communicate and influence them is a skill that can be transferred to concepts. The things outlined in this book need to be recognized for what value they can add to what you are attempting to accomplish in regards to making a transition and utilize that value to positively influence your mission. Respect the criteria found in Keeping It Real.

Conclusion

Be sure to take away the following points:

- Respecting accountability includes being accountable for your actions despite what other people are doing, getting away with, or how hypocritical they may appear.

- Adhering to the principles in this book without respect is an act rooted in futility.

- In this book, respect occurs when you show regard and consideration for the actors and circumstances that relate to the adherence of the previous five principles outlined above.

- Respect is a two-way street that is about showing regard and consideration, not about being scared or getting punked.

- Respect helps to build positive relationships.

Follow-Up

1. What does respect mean to you in regards to the four principles outlined so far in this book?

2. How can utilizing this principle help you have a successful future?

3. Do you think you have the success trait associated with this principle? If yes, how do you plan on utilizing that trait to make your transition successful? If not, how can you compensate for that shortfall in order to make your transition a success?

Final Word

Nothing is going to be perfect. In other words, you won't get any process right every time, nor will all of the components that make up a process be firing perfectly on all cylinders every time. However, you can have small victories. Those little successes can energize you and help you keep it moving forward.

Realizing that keeping it real is a process—not an event—is important. Processes sometimes don't produce any immediate rewards. That's why you have to stay focused and maintain stamina.

I can recall looking for a job while I was in work release with no success. I couldn't get a job flipping burgers. I was confused. Here I am with two bachelor's degrees, a certificate in computer support and repair indicating my computer literacy, a certificate in culinary arts from Ivy Tech, and I am ServSafe certified, which is a food safety management certificate from the National Restaurant Association. Yet, I still couldn't get a job at a fast food joint.

I was extremely excited when I got an interview for an account executive position at a logistics company. However, my bubble was destroyed when they shot me all the way down after they found out about my background. The rejection went on and on. Fortunately, I found a job, but it offered extremely low pay, and I was only getting between five and ten hours a week. The process wasn't paying off right then and there. I wanted to quit, I wanted to slang some dope, and I wanted to make it make sense at that moment. However, I held on, focused, worked hard, made good decisions, and eventually things started looking better and are steadily improving.

I don't always get all the things right but I do always make an effort. I obviously didn't get it right when I came across O.G., but it was a valuable learning experience. I even lost some momentum with my publishing business, because I am not having the success that I anticipated. I thought that if I built it, the readers and success will come. Not the case. As a result, I took my foot off the gas and stopped working on my business in the similar manner I did from the outset. My auntie even remarked saying, "You was on it at first, now…you are slacking!" However, I am regaining momentum and slowly but surely trying to realize my vision.

You will most likely hit rough spots, but you have to keep it moving, believing that success will soon come. Nothing occurs overnight, and there aren't any 'realize your vision' quick schemes that work; however, keeping it real does.

Set some goals and have faith in your ability to learn and accomplish the goals you have set. *Do not* allow your past to become an excuse for failure or worse not even trying. Instead, use it as an excuse for greatness.

Get your priorities in order and write them down to have something visual to reference. You do it when you make that grocery list, and that's nowhere near as important as this list.

Hold yourself accountable to everything on that list until it is time to make a new list of priorities that are worthy of someone with tremendous responsibilities.

Finally, respect everything and everyone. You never know what you will learn or how what you have learned will help you and those around you. In addition, you never know who you will come across, what their status is, or how you can make a positive impact on their life by giving them respect.

I will leave you with a quote from a guy who was offered money to murder me and later went to prison with a 110-year prison sentence, gave the time back, and got out only to be murdered. His is a story of tremendously high self-efficacy followed by an extremely low ability to prioritize, but that's an entire different book. He used to always say to me, "The hardest part about being real is keeping it real!"

APPENDIX

Priority Scale Picture and Example

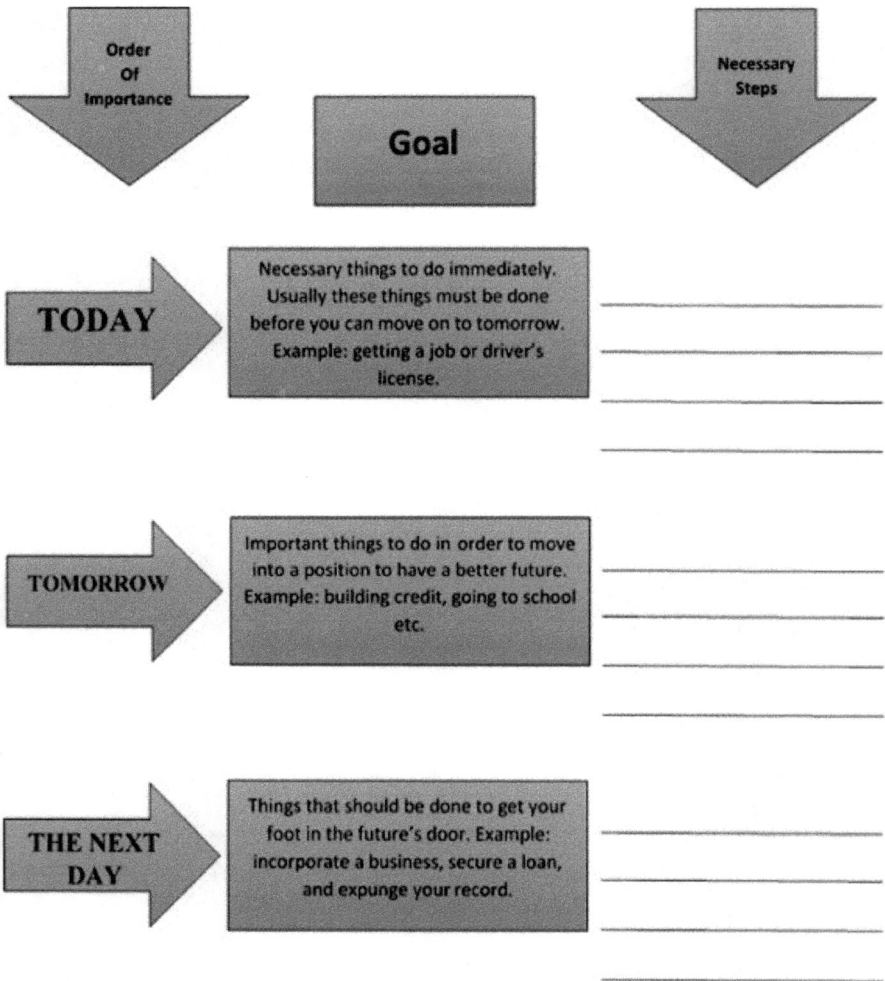

Order
Of
Importance

Necessary
Steps

Goal

TODAY

Necessary things to do immediately. Usually these things must be done before you can move on to tomorrow. Example: getting a job or driver's license.

_____
_____
_____
_____

TOMORROW

Important things to do in order to move into a position to have a better future. Example: building credit, going to school etc.

_____
_____
_____

THE NEXT DAY

Things that should be done to get your foot in the future's door. Example: incorporate a business, secure a loan, and expunge your record.

_____
_____
_____

Begin by determining your goal or goals.	Then determine what steps you need to take in order to ultimately reach those goals.	Next, determine in what order those steps should be taken. For example, you shouldn't get a car before you get a license so getting a license is more important than getting a car.
Order of Importance	**Goal:** To become a published author!	**Necessary Steps**
Today	Necessary things to do immediately. Usually these things must be done before you can move on to tomorrow. Example: getting a job or driver's license.	1. Find a job 2. Get driver's license 3. Open a bank account
Tommorrow	Important things to do in order to move into a position to have a better future. Example: building credit, going to school etc.	1. Begin saving money 2. get a secured credit card 3. Get a car
The Next Day	Things that should be done to get your foot in the future's door. Example: incorporate a business, secure a loan, and expunge your record.	1. Learn how to publish my own book 2. Get a financial coach 3. Create Ball Team Enterprise LLC.

The Keeping It Real Blue Print (example)

Goal

I see myself as a SUCCESFUL published author.

Goal Attainment

Today's goal

1. Find a job

2. Get driver's license

3. Open a bank account

Tomorrow's goal

1. Begin saving money

2. Get a secured credit card

3. Get a car

The next day's goal

1. Learn how to publish my own book

2. Get a financial coach

3. Create Ball Team Enterprise LLC.

Accountability

Owning up to what I did that landed me in prison and sharing my experience with the world as opposed to trying to hide it. That way I can get over the fact that I am a person with a conviction and so can those around me.

Responsibility

I have to be responsible for satisfying the terms of my parole, paying my bills on time, building my credit, and figuring out how to publish my own books and not wait for someone to do it for me.

Self-advocacy

I will become a successful published author who capitalizes on my mistakes and doesn't allow people or things from my past to keep me from realizing my goal. If you aren't helping me become that successful author we don't need to hang out and keep conversation and interaction limited at best.

Respect

I plan on utilizing respect by: respecting, not hiding my past; respecting my ability to learn and problem-solve to figure out how to be successful.

Author

Edward Ball is the founder of Ball Team Enterprise LLC. He founded this company to help people extract lessons from their mistakes and the mistakes of others and use those lessons as personal and professional development tools. Through his eBooks and other informational materials, he aims to help people be the best they can be. He spent fifteen years in prison and is an expert on making mistakes. After being sentenced to nearly forty years in prison, Mr. Ball earned two Bachelor's degrees, one in Liberal Arts-Human Interaction from Indiana State University and one in Organizational Management from Grace College. He extends the following offer to anyone with the ability and willingness to learn: Be better, do better…come learn with us, Ball Team Enterprise.

Connect with Edward:

- http://twitter.com/ballteamllc

- **ballteamenterprise.com**

- EdwardLBall.com

Other Ball Team Enterprise LLC Publications:

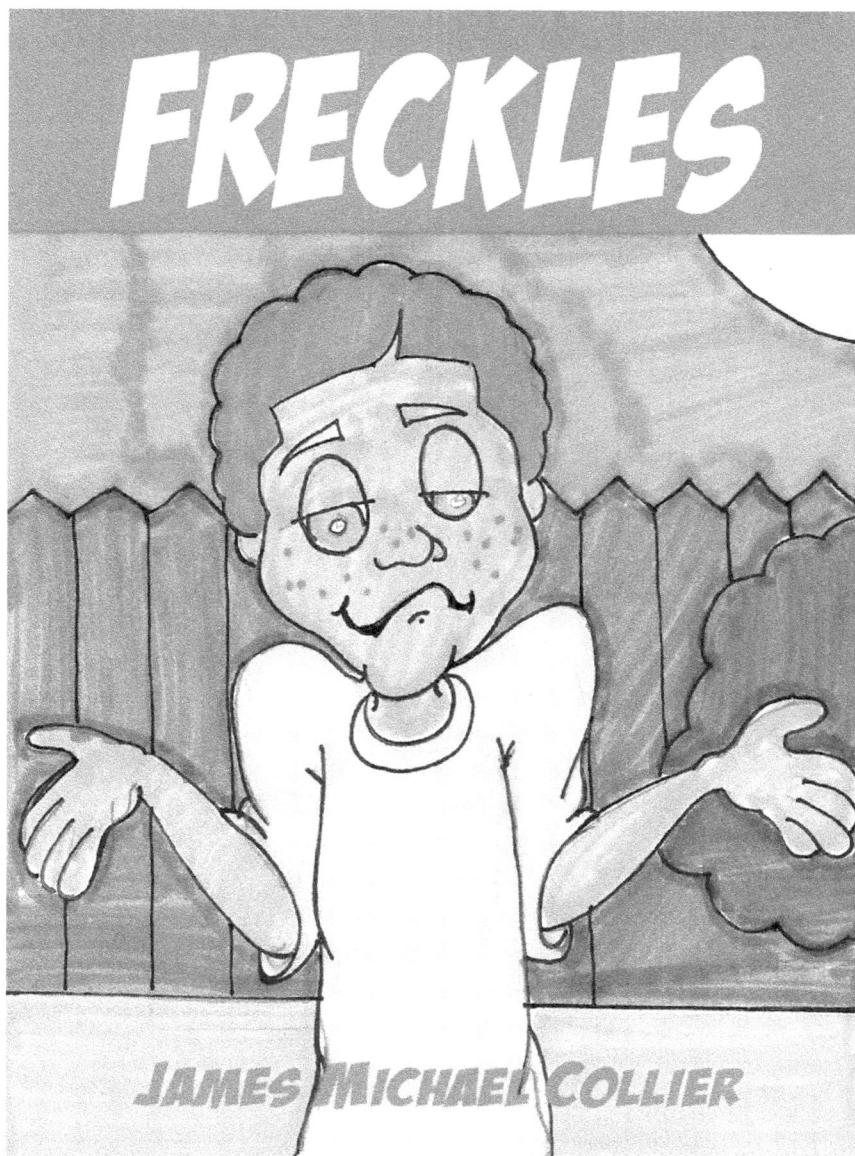

Other Books By Edward Ball

39 THINGS ABOUT LIFE I LEARNED IN PRISON

TURN MY MISTAKE INTO YOUR SUCCESS

EDWARD BALL

WHAT I LEARNED IN THE STREETS & PRISON

THAT CAN HELP YOU *WIN* AT THE GAME OF LIFE

BY

EDWARD BALL